POCKET ELIZABETH TAYLOR WISDOM

Witty quotes & wise words from a true icon

Pocket Elizabeth Taylor Wisdom

First published in 2018 by Hardie Grant Books, an imprint of
Hardie Grant Publishing

Hardie Grant Books (London)
5th and 6th Floors
52–54 Southwark Street
London SE1 1UN

Hardie Grant Books (Melbourne)
Building 1, 658 Church Street
Richmond, Victoria 3121

hardiegrantbooks.com

Text © Interplanet Productions, Limited
Cover Illustration © Michele Rosenthal

British Library Cataloguing-in-Publication Data. A catalogue
record for this book is available from the British Library.

ISBN: 978-1-78488-159-7

Publisher: Kate Pollard
Commissioning Editor: Kajal Mistry
Desk Editor: Molly Ahuja
Publishing Assistant: Eila Purvis
Design: Claire Warner Studio
Colour Reproduction by p2d
Printed and bound at Toppan Leefung, DongGuan City, China

POCKET
ELIZABETH TAYLOR
WISDOM

Witty quotes & wise words from a true icon

hardie grant books

CONTENTS

Self

"I've been lucky all my life. Everything was handed to me. Looks, fame, wealth, honors, love. But I've paid for that luck with disasters. Terrible illnesses, destructive addictions, broken marriages."

"I have made horrendous mistakes in my life, but I cannot blame them on anybody else. We all have to participate in our own downfalls."

"I am glad that in my life
I have never cut short my
emotions. The most awful
thing of all is to be numb."

"It is not true that I like animals more than people. But they come a very close second. There is no bullshit about them."

"I feel very adventurous. There are so many doors to be opened, and I'm not afraid to look behind them."

"I never think about
growing old; I barely think
about growing up."

"I don't dwell on the miserable. I skirt around that. Give it a wave. Wave goodbye and concentrate on the good things."

"I'm *not* a 'sex queen'
or a 'sex symbol'. I don't
think I *want* to be one...
sex symbol kind of suggests
bathrooms in hotels."

"I don't think I'm hedonistic,
but I'm certainly *not*
masochistic."

"Watching my children is like watching wonderful flowers opening to the sun."

"As a mother, my main ambition was to give my kids their privacy... and a right to their own separate lives."

"I've been through it all, baby.
I'm Mother Courage. I'll
be dragging my sable coat
behind me in old age."

– ELIZABETH ON –

Beauty

"All I see in the mirror every morning is a face that needs washing."

"I've always hated having my picture taken. I think still photographs are rather vain."

"I read in the paper that someone had a fat picture of me on her refrigerator door to keep her from eating, and I said to myself, well, if it helps her it ought to help me."

"When I'm sick I always look healthy. I get this pink glow in my cheeks. Everyone says, 'You look really well.' I've got a bloody brain tumor! I want some sympathy please."

"The kind of beauty where you're afraid to smile too much is such a bore."

"As a girl, my mother told me I'm nice looking and that I have pretty eyes, but it's not your eyes... it's the expression behind your eyes that will make you truly beautiful."

"I've always been very aware of the inner me that has nothing to do with the physical me."

"What you are is what others perceive of you. Who you are is what you perceive of yourself."

Activism
& Giving

"Nothing will raise your self-esteem as much as helping others. It will make you like yourself more and make you more likable."

"I will not be silenced
and I will not give up and
I will not be ignored."

"You don't need
an award to be, or not
be, a humanitarian."

"I will remain here as rowdy an activist as I have to be and God willing, for as long as I have to be!"

"I call upon to you to draw from the depths of your being to prove that we are a human race. To prove that our love outweighs our need to hate. That our compassion is more compelling than our need to blame. That our sensitivity to those in need is stronger than our greed...

...That our ability to reason overcomes our fear and that at the end of each of our lives, we can look back and be proud that we have treated others with the kindness, dignity and respect that every human being deserves"

"Every breath you take today should be with someone else in mind."

"This town (Hollywood) and Washington D.C., are the biggest bullshit towns in the world. They both have picket fences surrounding them, and they live and feed off of people."

– ELIZABETH ON –

Love &
Marriage

"I am a very committed wife.
And I should be committed,
too — for being married
so many times."

"I think marriage does give a sense of oneness that just being together can't."

"If it is love, it must encompass everything. The faults as well as the things you are proud of, and one has to be tolerant of one's intolerancies."

"If I love someone,
I love them always."

"I've never asked for alimony in my life."

"I think having a fight,
an out and out outrageous,
ridiculous fight is one
of the greatest exercises
in marital togetherness."

"There can be no love
without respect."

"If you hear of me getting married [again], slap me!"

"How can anything bad come out of love? The bad stuff comes out of mistrust, misunderstanding and God knows from hate and from ignorance."

"Those against gay marriages say marriage should only be between a man and a woman. God… I of all people know that that doesn't always work!"

"When I have fallen in love
it's always ended up being
a marrying kind of love."

"Every day we need to tell someone we love them. Touch them. Thank them for being. It's so important."

– ELIZABETH ON –

Fame

"To my kids I'm not Elizabeth Taylor at all; I'm not anybody other than mum."

"I saw the difference between my image and my real self... I was a person before I was in films, and whatever the public thought of me, I knew who I really was."

"The public takes an animal delight in putting somebody at the top and then tearing them into little bits. But I have never in my life believed in fighting back to 'cure' my public image."

On using her fame to draw attention to the AIDS crisis in the early '80's: "I wanted to retire, but the tabloids wouldn't let me. So I thought, if you're going to screw me over, I'll use you."

"I haven't done a film for years.
I've done everything I can
to give up my fame, but my
fame won't give me up."

"I think there are times when being famous is useful... and if I or any other celebrity can help, then we should do everything we can. That's the only reason for being famous."

"The Elizabeth Taylor who's famous, the one on film, really has no depth or meaning to me. She's a totally superficial working thing, a commodity. I really don't know what the ingredients of the image are exactly — just that it makes money."

"I owe the public who pays to see me on the screen the best performance I can give. As to how I live my personal life, my responsibility is to the people directly involved with me."

– ELIZABETH ON –

Acting

"I found quite early that
I couldn't act as a puppet...
and that I did my best work
by being guided, not by
being forced."

"AIDS is real life. Acting is make-believe. One is real tragedy and one is pretend."

"I don't feel like I'm really a part of Hollywood. But I never really was. I've always kept myself on the fringes."

"I never had an acting lesson.
I don't know how to act per se.
I just developed as an actress.
Acting is instinctive with me.
It's mostly concentration —
making yourself be the part
you're playing."

"I was constricted by shyness —
I still am — and acting meant
I could be at least behind
someone else's façade."

"I think film acting can be art, and certainly the camera can move in and grab hold of your mind — so the emotion has got to be there behind your eyes, behind your heart."

"I was pronounced dead.
I've read my own obituaries.
They were the best reviews
I've ever had."

"Some of my best leading men have been dogs and horses."

Jewels & Presents

"You can't cry on
a diamond's shoulder,
and diamonds won't
keep you warm at night,
but they're sure fun
when the sun shines!"

"Mike (Todd) loved spoiling me and I adored receiving presents — I mean, I love presents. There is certainly nothing blasé about me in that area."

"My mind goes
buzzing off to jewellery
all the time."

"As I look at my jewels,
I realise what a lucky
girl I am."

"I adore wearing gems, but not because they are mine. You can't possess radiance, you can only admire it."

"I've never thought of my jewellery as trophies.
I'm here to take care of it and love it, for we are only temporary custodians of beauty."

"I never planned to acquire a lot of jewels or a lot of husbands."

"I think the most exciting present I ever received was when I was 13, after I made *National Velvet* and the studio gave me the horse. That just blew my mind!"

– ELIZABETH ON –

Life

"If you don't have darkness, you don't know light."

"I haven't had a quiet life.
I've lived dangerously.
Sometimes disaster has
come at me like a train. I've
almost died several times…
yet some instinct, some inner
force has always saved me,
dragging me back just as
the train whooshed past."

"I believe in life and I'll fight for it. I believe you have to put up your dukes and fight, even if you don't know what you're fighting against."

"We all have to participate in our own downfalls, and it doesn't absolve you to cop a plea by throwing mud on other people. The one who throws the mud is always reduced."

"You cannot have passion of any kind unless you have compassion."

"Excuses cannot
absolve you, and they
are so undignified."

"I believe people are like rocks formed by the weather... by experience, by heartache, by grief, by mistakes, by guilt, by shame... how do you become a full-fledged human being without taking the brunt head on?"

"Pour yourself a drink,
put on some lipstick and
pull yourself together."

"It is strange that the
years can teach us patience;
that the shorter our time,
the greater our capacity
for waiting."

"In the end, it really only matters what you think of yourself."

— SOURCES —

Backstage at the Academy Awards, 1993 – pp. 67

Barbara Walters Oscar Night Special, 1998 – pp. 45

Elizabeth Taylor, by Elizabeth Taylor, 1964 – pp. 9, 10, 11, 77, 91, 92

Entertainment Tonight, 2007 – pp. 14, 18, 78

GLAAD Media Awards, 2000 – pp. 35, 50, 51

Interview Magazine, Feb. 2007 – pp. 22, 34, 56

Last public words from Elizabeth Taylor via Twitter, 2010 – pp. 38

Life Magazine, 1964 – pp. 15, 58, 62, 89

Life Magazine, 1997 – pp. 8, 25, 53, 87, 88

Liz Smith Interview, 1993 – pp. 86

Look Magazine, 1961 – pp. 17, 23, 69

My Love Affair With Jewellery – pp. 76, 79, 80, 81, 82

Premiere Magazine, 1992 – pp. 16, 39, 68

Press Conference on AIDS – pp. 33, 61

Rolling Stone Lost Interview 1987 – pp. 28, 63, 66, 70, 71, 90

Speaking to Congress for AIDS funding – pp. 33

The David Frost Show, 1970 – pp. 44

The Johnny Carson Show, 1992 – pp. 72, 83

Upon receiving the Jean Hersholt Humanitarian Oscar, 1993 – pp. 36, 37

Vanity Fair, December 1985 – pp. 24, 46

Vanity Fair, November 1992 – pp. 59

20/20 Interview with Barbara Walters – pp. 49, 52

60 Minutes, 1970 – pp. 47